LIFE SKILLS
FOR TEENAGE GIRLS

How to Be Healthy, Avoid Drama, Manage Money, Be Confident, Fix Your Car, Unclog Your Sink, and Other Important Skills Teen Girls Should Know!

By
KAREN HARRIS

FREE BONUS

SCAN TO GET OUR NEXT BOOK FOR FREE!

TABLE OF CONTENTS

CHAPTER ONE:
GOOD FINANCIAL WELLNESS FROM THE START

Growing up, you might not realize how important it is to pay attention to your finances. But, if you can get it right from the start, you'll be well on your way to financial success. One of the first things to decide is where to keep your money.

Initially, when you might not have much more than an allowance or cash from odd jobs, you might simply keep it with you. That's perfectly fine. Even when you keep your money as cash, there are some things you can do to ensure it's safe.

First, make sure to store it in a safe place. This might be a drawer in your bedroom or in your purse. Be mindful of who knows where you keep your money and monitor it to make sure no one has reached into your secret stash. It might not seem like a big deal now, but it's important to know where your money is, how much you have, and how other people respond to your money.

For instance, do you have one friend who never seems to have their own money but always wants to go shopping or out to eat with your group of friends? It's nice to help out every once in a while, but after a bit it can become frustrating. After all, you're not working and saving your money for them. You have plans for that money.

Once you've established a larger amount of money, it's time to consider other options for safekeeping. A few years ago, your options were fewer. Basically, you would choose a bank in your hometown. Now, there are many online banking options as well. Almost all banks, online or in-person, allow you to open a checking or savings account with little to no fees. This is the type of account you want when you're starting out. There are also some online banks that will offer you a higher interest rate for your deposit.

Where you live will determine what your options are. Unfortunately, you might not have easy access to a bank. You might not be able to get there, or you may simply live in an area without a bank right down the street. In this instance, online banking will be the way to go.

If saving money is your goal (it should be your goal for at least some of your money!), you'll want to work with the bank that offers you the highest return on your investment.

Of course, all of this also depends on how you're receiving your money. If you're receiving cash payments, an in-person bank is likely your best option.

If you receive your money through direct deposit, several options open up. In fact, there are many employers who have their own system set up. You might get a card through your employer that can act as a debit card and has your check directly deposited to it. Or, your company may have an app, such as Gusto, where you can opt to have the whole check or part of a check deposited. These options make deciding where to store your money easy as the question is answered for you.

Understand, though, that you can bypass these options from your employer and opt for a more traditional bank if you wish. This offers several advantages if you're unsure which to choose. For instance, for most of these apps or debit card options, you may get paid sooner than your actual pay date—up to two days earlier in a lot of cases. This is a nice perk. You'll want to make sure your money is easy to access if you choose to stay with these options. If you choose to use an app, they may send you a debit card to use. It can be used at ATMs, but pay attention to whether there are ATM fees, as these can add up.

If you choose the traditional route and keep your money in a bank, make sure to do your research. For most banks, you will need an adult officially on the account with you until you turn eighteen.

Once you've established which bank you're using, it's time to discuss safety once again. Whether you're using the debit card offered to you by your employer, or the one from your brand new checking account, knowing where it is at all times is crucial. That card is linked to vital information about you, not to mention it holds the key to all your money.

Simply leaving it lying around for anyone to see can cause issues. You need to protect your card, account, and pin numbers. Do your best not to write down any information or even leave it on your phone. Your bank might be able to protect you if someone gets a hold of the information and uses your card, but getting things reversed can be frustrating. Plus, this may put a pause on your money, meaning you won't be able to access it when needed. This pause typically only lasts a few days, but it's still annoying.

You will receive a four-number password for the card associated with your account, and you'll register with your email address and a password to be able access your account online. The passwords shouldn't be something easily guessed, like 1234 or your birth month and date. Yes, these are easy for you to remember, but anyone wanting access to your money can figure them out pretty quickly.

When creating your account password make sure to use a long password. String together a few nonsense words while sprinkling in numbers and a few symbols. Do not make it obvious or use personal information. For example, using the password OvertheRainbow.#43 is much better than using your favorite color and birth year or something similar.

You can see in the example that both lower case and upper case letters were used, along with symbols and numbers. This is a vital step in password creation. Once you've created a unique password, you might find it easier to use that same password for everything. This is a mistake. Easier? Yes. But it's also easier for anyone trying to steal your information.

It's important to change your password a few times a year. Some even say every month is a good idea. Do your best not to reuse old passwords, although this might be tempting. If you're using public wi-fi, make sure to clear your cache and browsing history. On your phone, take advantage of security measures, such as fingerprint scans or other biometric options. This keeps your account and other information more protected.

And don't add your best friend's fingerprint simply because they like to get in and play music from your playlist. It's important for you to maintain security from the start.

IS CREDIT REALLY THAT IMPORTANT?

One hundred percent, yes. No one talks about credit as you're growing up, but it's a topic that should be introduced at an early age. Credit is the key to affording the life you hope to live, retiring at a decent age, and decreasing stress as you become an adult.

Getting out of credit problems can be time-consuming, stressful, and difficult. Sound scary? It won't be if you handle your finances well from the beginning. Right now, with your part-time job, this might not sound like it's that big of a deal. But take it from someone who received their first credit card at eighteen and is still in debt thirty years later. Credit is a big deal.

Once you turn eighteen, credit card offers might start rolling in. They're not as easy to get as they used to be, but you can still rack up a hefty debt in just one trip to the mall. Credit serves its purpose. It allows you to purchase items you need and pay for them in smaller increments over time. The key word there is "need." Credit is for things you need, not for things you want.

For instance, you may need a car to get to your job. If you've saved your money and can pay for it outright, that's fantastic! Kudos to you. But you may need to get a car loan to help pay for anything over the down payment you provide. This is a great way to earn credit and show that you are financially mature.

Paying your loan payments on time and consistently will improve your credit score and allow you to purchase even larger things later, like a house. The minute you get behind on your payments, though, that credit score starts to decrease.

Let's step back a minute and start even smaller than a car. Your first credit card might be for your favorite store or a general credit card offered through your bank. With a limit of $500, it may seem like you have extra money to spend on that phone you've been eyeing. But, do you really need the phone? If the answer is an eye roll and an "of course I do," wait for a week or two to see if the reaction is still as strong. Avoiding impulse buying is one of the first tips for building a strong credit history.

That being said, if you want to increase your credit score (and you do in order to afford things like a house or a car) you will need to use the credit that is offered to you. The best thing to do is use it for something you already have the money for.

For instance, let's say you go to your favorite store with the intent to buy a sweatshirt with the cash you have. The clerk offers a store credit card for a discount on your purchase. You apply and are approved. Wonderful! You can opt to put it on the credit card right then. You can also then pay off the card right away. Or you can wait until the billing information arrives in the mail and pay it off then. The important thing is to pay it off each month. Don't put more on your card than you can afford to pay off at the end of the month.

Credit offers newfound freedom that can be incredibly tempting, but it can also cause problems when you charge more than you can afford. If you've spent $500 on something and can't pay it off right away, you are allowed to make payments. But, your credit account accrues interest, and depending on how long it takes you to pay off, you could end up paying $1000 for that $500 purchase. At that point, you're essentially giving away your hard-earned money.

READING YOUR CREDIT REPORT

Where Can You Find Your Report?

You are allowed a free copy of your credit report from all three major credit bureaus once per year at AnnualCreditReport.com. If you want to see all three reports at once, it will cost $19.95. If you'd rather stagger the reports over time, that's fine—you'll still be able to receive a free report from each bureau every twelve months.

Where to Find Your Credit Score?

The Fair Credit Reporting Act mandates that the big three credit bureaus (Equifax, Experian, and TransUnion) provide all consumers a free copy of their credit reports once every twelve months. You can get your report from each bureau by visiting AnnualCreditReport.com. Be sure to check all three—they're legally required to have similar information on file. Many financial apps will also provide a fairly accurate estimate of your credit score based upon your current debt to income ratio, the length of your credit history, and the number of derogatory marks you have against you for things such as late payments.

How Do I Get Mistakes Fixed?

If you find a mistake on your report, don't just assume it will be corrected when you ask for an update later on down the road. Call the reporting agency directly and ask them to fix it right away; otherwise, they may wait until the next time they send out their monthly updates before making any changes at all. Requesting changes can take some time, and you might have to provide documentation, but it's worth it to get something taken off your report that doesn't belong to you.

Now that we've talked about finding the right checking account, credit cards, and credit reporting, it's time to talk about creating a budget and saving your money as well.

CREATING A BUDGET

You may wonder why you need to create a budget if you're only making a little bit of money, but learning how to budget from the start will help you make it a habit in the future.

When you are creating your first budget, it's important to plan for the future. You need to think about how much money you will require to cover your expenses each month and how long you will need that money to last. You also need to think about your short-term and long-term financial goals.

If you're not sure where to start, there are many online resources available that can help you create a budget that works for you. The most important thing is to be honest with yourself about your spending. And remember to make sure that your budget allows you enough flexibility to cover unexpected expenses.

If you find that you are not able to stick to your budget, don't be afraid to make changes. The most important thing is that you are proactive about your finances and are working toward a goal.

Make sure to set aside money in your budget to have fun as well. This will make it easier to stick to your budget, and it won't feel like earning money is all work and no fun.

How Much Should You Save Each Paycheck?

When it comes to saving, there is no one-size-fits-all answer. What's important is that you save *something*, even if it's a small amount at first. You can gradually increase your savings as you grow more comfortable with budgeting and see how much money you have left over each month.

To figure out how much money to save from your paycheck, start by looking at your long-term goals. Do you want to find a place to live on your own? Save for a car? Go to a concert this summer? Once you know what you're saving for, you can come up with a target amount and work backward to figure out how much you will need to save each month.

If your goal is to build an emergency fund, try to save at least three to six months' worth of living expenses.

Remember earlier when impulse buying was introduced? The same advice that applies to using your credit card applies here too. Yes, you have the cash, but is the purchase a need or is it a want? Can you wait a few days to see if you still really want the item? While you're waiting, consider how you will use it, or search for the same thing at a lower cost.

Many times when we wait, we realize we never really wanted the item at all. If you've already purchased it, it's too late.

Most people have a savings account in the same bank where they have their checking account. You can do this as well, but pay attention to interest rates. If you can gain while saving, that's the best choice for you.

You might also take the chance to learn a bit about the stock market while you're young and it's a bit less risky. There are plenty of apps that allow you to start small and learn while you go. Take advantage of these options. Starting now can build you an excellent nest-egg for when you get older.

You should also inquire about retirement options at your job, even if you're only part-time. It's never too soon to start saving for the future.

SHOPPING SMART

When you're looking to save money, the best way to do so is by shopping efficiently. This means taking the time to learn about which stores have the best deals and which coupon apps to use. Here are a few tips on how to find the best deals when shopping.

The first step is to figure out which stores have the best deals. A great way to do this is by checking out store circulars. This is where stores advertise their sales and discounts. You can usually find these circulars in your local paper or online.

Another great way to find deals is by using coupon apps. There are a number of different apps available, but some of our favorites include Coupon Sherpa, RetailMeNot, and Checkout 51. These apps allow you to search for coupons for specific stores or brands.

Pay attention when buying in bulk. Do the math and figure out if buying in bulk is worth it. You also need to consider if you have the space to store more items than what you need currently. Sometimes more is not better.

Most stores will send you regular coupons if you provide them with an email. It's a good idea to have an email specifically for such purposes. Your regular email will quickly fill up if you use that one.

It's also good to understand that you don't have to buy something simply because it's on sale. Yes, if you've been waiting for it to go on sale and you've wanted it for a long time, take advantage and enjoy the purchase. But, if you've never considered the purple polka-dotted llama lamp before, chances are you're just reacting to the excitement of the sale.

Last but not least, make a list. Go shopping with your list and don't veer from it. Also, if you're grocery shopping, don't go while you're hungry or rushed. You can end up making impulse decisions that waste money and food that will sit in your kitchen until it's time to throw it out.

APPLYING FOR YOUR FIRST LOAN

You've saved your money, and you're working hard. Now it's time to apply for your first loan. You might be surprised to find out that saving money for your loan is one of the first steps.

When you're getting ready to take out your first loan, it's important to save as much money as you can and create a budget. Budgeting for your loan payments is key because you don't want to be struggling to make ends meet every month.

Try to set aside a little money each month so you can easily make your loan payments on time. And don't forget to factor in all of your other expenses too. You don't want to be overspending each month just because you have a loan payment. By being smart about your finances and preparing ahead of time, you'll make taking out your first loan much easier on yourself.

When you have a few loan payments set aside, you will have a loan nest-egg to reach from in case of an emergency. Planning ahead will keep you on the path to financial freedom and keep stress about your expenses at bay.

Pay attention to the interest rates on loans. Can you pay additional money each payment to lessen the amount of the loan? Even paying every other week rather than monthly will cut down on your payments. The quicker you pay off the loan, the less money you will need to pay back.

You don't have to get a loan from your bank, although that might be easier. It's important to shop around, though, like any other shopping you do. You want to find the best rates and the best payments that work for you.

When making a big purchase that requires a loan, consider everything else that goes into that purchase as well. Let's say the loan is for a car. You need to consider the cost of maintenance, gasoline, and insurance for the car as well. All these bills go into the total cost of the car. You may be able to afford a $300 car payment, but once you add on these other things, you might find yourself struggling at the month's end. Living within your means is a good lesson to always carry with you.

CHAPTER TWO:
IS IT TIME
FOR A CAR?

Buying your first car is a milestone that can be both exciting and daunting. It's an important step toward adulthood, but it comes with a lot of financial responsibility.

Here are some things to consider when getting your first car loan.

WHAT IS
A CO-SIGNER?

Lenders may require that someone co-sign the loan with you if you don't have any credit history or have bad credit. A co-signer is another person who takes responsibility for repaying the loan if you don't pay it off as agreed. If you don't make payments on time, the lender can pursue legal action against both parties involved in the contract.

Co-signers are typically family members or friends who have good credit and can help you build your own credit history by adding their names as well as their income to your loan application. Co-signing for someone else can help them get approved for a larger amount than they could otherwise afford alone—but this also means the payment goes up, so consider this when offered a larger loan.

DECIDE HOW MUCH YOU CAN AFFORD

Before you shop for your first car, figure out how much of an auto loan you can handle. If you're paying for college or other expenses in addition to the down payment and monthly payments, that could affect how much money you should borrow. Remember—add in gas, maintenance, and insurance as well. Having a car isn't any fun when you can't drive it around.

Always remember that there are other options besides taking out a loan. You could choose to save up money and buy a cheaper car out of pocket. Aside from keeping the above factors in mind, you should also consider the risks of purchasing a vehicle outside of a dealership.

Although sales representatives at dealerships are notorious for glazing over issues with their merchandise and upselling as much as they can, buying from a private owner can include the same risks with less of a support system. If the private owner lies about the vehicle, there is no contract to help you take action against them. With that said, if you are smart about your purchase, you can save a lot of money by purchasing a used vehicle from a private owner.

CHOOSING
YOUR CAR

There's no reason to buy a vehicle that doesn't match your needs. If a certain brand or style doesn't fit, don't buy it just because it looks cool or seems like something every high schooler has to own. You might end up having buyer's remorse later on—not to mention having trouble reselling the vehicle when it comes time to trade up or sell!

More importantly, be realistic. If this is your first car, you will most likely make mistakes with it. For this reason, it might be better to start with a cheaper car and buy your dream car later.

Have you looked at different dealerships online?

Shop around. Look into local dealerships or private sellers, or check out websites like Craigslist or Autotrader to find used cars. Get quotes from several dealerships and independent sellers, and compare them before making a decision.

Can you get the loan you need?

Get pre-approved for financing. This will help you negotiate better terms with the seller because they won't have to worry about whether you can afford the car or not.

Do you know someone who is good with cars?

Make sure the car is in good working order before making an offer on it—this includes checking the fluids and oil levels, examining the brakes (don't forget about brake pads!), looking for leaks under the vehicle, etc. If you're buying from a dealership, you should get a warranty of sorts, but you still want to make sure you're getting the best deal possible.

MAINTAINING
YOUR NEW CAR

Now that you have a car, you want to make sure it stays in good condition. If the car came with a warranty, that's great. Some dealerships will even offer discounted oil changes if you bring the car to them. This is a good idea since you've already worked with the team.

Read your manual and talk with the mechanic who services the car. How often do you need an oil change? Newer cars can last longer, but older cars typically need the oil changed every three thousand miles.

In a lot of cases, you can change your oil easily, but depending on the car's age, you might not be able to change it on your own.

Check your car's owner's manual or search for a video to show you how to check your engine's oil. In general, you should check your oil level every time you fill up your gas tank. Most cars require between five and seven quarts of oil, but this will vary depending on the make and model.

To check the oil level, find the dipstick (usually located near the engine), pull it out, wipe it off with a cloth, reinsert it fully, and then pull it out again. The oil level should be at or slightly below the full mark on the dipstick. If it's not, add more oil accordingly.

Your manual should tell you what type of oil your car takes. Even if you're checking your oil regularly, you still need to have it changed at the correct mileage. There are other things that are part of an oil change in addition to just adding oil. If you decide to learn how to change your oil, the steps are quite simple. If you have a friend or family member who knows how to do it, have them walk you through it until you're comfortable doing it on your own.

The first step to changing your oil is to gather your supplies. You'll need:

- An oil change kit (you can get one at any auto parts store)
- A drain pan (to catch the dirty oil)
- A funnel (to make it easier to pour the new oil in)
- A clean shop rag or old towel (for wiping off things you don't want dirty)

The steps for changing your car's oil are fairly simple:

1. Make sure the engine is cool and that you have a jack, lug wrench, and oil pan.
2. Loosen the lug nuts on the wheels, jack up the car, remove the wheel nuts and wheel, and set them aside.
3. Drain the old oil into the oil pan, replace the drain plug, replace the wheel and wheel nuts, lower the car to the ground, and add fresh oil.
4. Finally, dispose of used motor oil responsibly.

If changing your oil yourself doesn't appeal to you, or you have a newer car that can make it more difficult, that's okay! There are trained specialists who are more than willing to do it for you. Plus, they will check your fluids, windshield wipers, tires, and lights to make sure everything is in good working order.

You can go to the dealership where you purchased the car if they have a service center, or there are quick oil change businesses in many cities and towns. Before going, take note of what type of oil you need. Most businesses will walk you through what they're doing so you understand the process.

They will also ask if you need windshield wipers or new air filters. By checking your manual, you will have a good idea of when your filters need to be replaced, and being aware of whether you need new wipers is easy as well.

There are other places to get both of these items, and you might find they are cheaper elsewhere. Many parts stores will even install your wiper blades for you with purchase.

OTHER MAINTENANCE ISSUES

Every other time you get your oil changed, opt to have your tires rotated as well. Or, if your oil needs to be changed less often, you may have them rotated each time.

It is a good idea to rotate your tires every five thousand miles. Tire rotation helps to even out the wear on your tires so they last longer. When you have your tires rotated, the technician will also check the air pressure and alignment.

Many cars now tell you exactly what they need and when they need regular maintenance so you can stay on top of everything. In order to do that, you need to find a mechanic you trust who doesn't mind spending time explaining things to you. That mechanic might not be at the dealership, but you might find them at a neighborhood shop.

There are air filters that will need to be changed, as you read earlier, as well as the windshield wipers. But also make sure to take a look at your manual and find out where your fuses are. Much like the fuses in a house, your car has fuses too.

There are many things you can handle yourself when it comes to car maintenance, such as changing bulbs or refilling fluids. Take the time to understand everything your car needs, and you will feel more comfortable when you seek outside help.

FINDING
A MECHANIC

The first step to finding a good mechanic is to find out if they are honest. You can do this by asking them questions about their past experiences and how they became a mechanic. You should also ask them if they have any recommendations for you to take your car to other mechanics or auto shops.

Looking at their website or online reviews to see what others say about the quality of their work and how long it took them to finish the job will also tell you a lot about their work ethic. Look at the prices of their services and compare them with other mechanics in your area.

The next step is to find out if they are qualified enough to work on your car. You can do this by asking them about the training and certifications that they received from schools, colleges, or other organizations within their field of expertise.

If you have purchased an older car that needs repair, then you should find out if the mechanic has experience repairing older models as well as newer models. This will help ensure that your car is repaired properly without causing any damage or problems in the future due to improper repairs. Inexperienced technicians might not know how older cars operate properly when performing repairs on them.

The best case scenario is that someone in your family or friend group has a mechanic they recommend. This can make your choice much easier. Still, you don't have to go with their mechanic, especially if it doesn't feel right after meeting with them.

Remember, this car is an investment and most likely your first big purchase. You have the right to ask questions and decide how to handle repairs and maintenance. Yes, you should take the mechanic's advice, but it's okay to ask for a second opinion if something seems off.

LEARNING TO DRIVE A STICK SHIFT (MANUAL TRANSMISSION)

Even though automatic cars are more practical, learning how to drive a manual car can be useful.

Since automatic car transmissions are more complex and have more parts and functions that can fail, manual automobile transmissions can be less expensive to maintain and replace.

Manual vehicles are also more common in some regions of the world. Knowing how to drive one can be useful when you travel.

If an emergency arises, manual car driving skills can be extremely useful. Imagine needing to get to a hospital, or to safety and only having a manual car to drive. At least knowing the basics will get you where you need to go.

Below you'll find a rough step-by-step guide on what to do if you need to drive this type of car. Taking a driving class that gives you experience as well as one-on-one instruction is a good idea if you truly want to know how to drive a stick shift.

- Turn the engine on.
- Push the clutch pedal (the pedal on the left) down.
- Move the gear stick into first gear.
- Use your right foot to lightly press down on the accelerator, increasing engine revs slightly.
- Use your left foot to slowly lift the clutch pedal until it starts to vibrate (this is sometimes known as the "bite point").
- Remove the handbrake, allowing the car to move slowly.
- Increase your revs while taking your foot off the clutch, using only the accelerator pedal to move.

Once you start driving around, there are a few things you'll need to know beyond road rules and how to drive.

First, it's important to make sure your car is always road ready. Make sure you have gas and proper air pressure in your tires. When you first start driving, it's a good idea to have an emergency kit in your car. A few things to include in the kit are listed below.

- A spare tire that is well inflated, a wheel wrench, and a jack

26

- Jumper cables
- Toolbox or a multifunctional utility tool
- Batteries and a flashlight
- Reflective triangles and brightly colored clothing to increase the visibility of your car
- Compass
- Gauze, tape, bandages, antibiotic cream, aspirin, a blanket, non-latex gloves, scissors, hydrocortisone, a thermometer, tweezers, and an instant cold compress (often included in a first aid kit)
- Foods that aren't perishable but are high in energy, including unsalted nuts, dried fruit, and hard candies
- Drinking water
- A reflective vest to wear in case you have to walk to find aid
- Cell phone charger for the car
- Fire extinguisher
- Rain gear
- A snow brush, shovel, windshield washer fluid, warm clothing, cat litter for traction, and blankets

Not all of these things will be needed depending on the climate you live in. You can usually buy a bundle at the store for a general-purpose emergency car kit. A great skill to have, besides learning how to drive a manual car, is knowing how to get unstuck if you and your car get stuck somewhere.

The following graphic can help you get out of most jams when you find that your tires are stuck and you can't move.

The first thing you should do in situations like this, of course, is to make sure it's safe to get out of the car.

Then, you can check to see what you're stuck on and if there are any other objects blocking you from moving. If there are, you will need to remove them first. If not, follow the graph depending on how you're stuck. It might be mud, snow, or sand that's getting you down.

No matter what, safety should always be on your mind.

UNDERSTANDING
YOUR CAR

There is a reason that cars come with owner's manuals. They tell you everything you need to know about your car, including how to fix small issues and what warning signs to be mindful of. Some cars can alert you to low tire pressure, while others may have crash detection installed.

When you first start driving your car, you'll need to make sure you understand how to operate the lights, windshield wipers, and more. Figuring these things out while driving isn't a good idea. Take the time to look at your manual when you get the car, so you're not taken by surprise.

You'll also want to figure out how the temperature system works, including how to defrost your windows and where your fuses are. The fuses allow different systems to operate within your car. If your dash lights aren't working, it might be a fuse issue.

Knowing your car inside and out will ensure you're safer on the road.

CHANGING
A TIRE

There are services that will come to change your tire for you, but they might be costly and take time to get to you. There's no shame in using these services, and they might be the best option for you.

Still, it's a good idea to understand the steps to change your tire if you get a flat. If you find yourself in a situation where you are the one who needs to change the tire, the best case scenario is that you've practiced beforehand. The next best scenario is that you have phone service and can look up a video to learn how to complete the task.

The steps are fairly simple, but they're not easy for everyone to do. It's a good idea to know who to call if your car needs to be towed. Make sure your car insurance covers towing as well.

Steps to change your tire:
1. Find a safe place to pull over.
2. Turn on your hazard lights.
3. Put on your emergency brake.
4. Get all your materials ready. Tire changing supplies should be in your trunk.
5. Loosen the lug nuts.
6. Jack the car off the ground.
7. Remove lug nuts and tire.

8. Place the spare tire on the car.
9. Replace the lug nuts.
10. Lower the car so that the tires just touch the ground.
11. Tighten every other lug nut.
12. Completely lower the vehicle.
13. Tighten the lug nuts the rest of the way.

You can put your old tire and tools back in the trunk and head to a dealership, tire shop, or mechanic to assess what is wrong with your tire. You shouldn't drive more than fifty miles on a spare tire.

When you start driving more, it's a good idea to familiarize yourself with a navigation app. Make sure that whatever app you use will talk to you. It's not safe for you be looking down at your phone while trying to figure out where the next turn is. Rely on the communication of the app to get you where you need to be.

What happens if you don't have service? How will you know where to go? You have a few options. It might be helpful for you to keep a map in your glove box at all times. Make sure you know how to use this map in a pinch.

Another good idea when going anywhere new is to copy the directions to your phone or print out the directions to take with you. There are times when the navigational apps on our phones get things wrong.

CHAPTER THREE:
A CRASH COURSE IN HYGIENE

HAIR CARE 101

Did you know that not everyone needs the same hair care? Some people need to wash their hair every other day while other people need it less often. It all depends on the texture and needs of your hair type.

As a rule of thumb, if your hair is thick and textured, you only need to wash your hair once every seven to ten days unless you are more active. In that case, you can wash your hair every four to five days.

If you have finer hair, you should stick to washing your hair every two to three days.

The texture of your hair also dictates the type of hair products you use. Talk with your friends and family to see what products they use. When it comes to biological family, your hair needs might be similar to theirs due to your genes.

If you're standing in the middle of the shampoo aisle and you're not sure which way to go, follow this simple guide.

Use a light clarifying shampoo if your hair is fine or you can hardly see or feel a single strand between your fingertips.

Look for something hydrating if you have thick or coarse hair.

If you have colored hair, seek a product that is color-safe and won't wash your hair dye out every time.

Look for a clarifying shampoo for bleached hair to avoid unwelcome yellow tones.

If you aren't sure what type of hair you have, here's a little tip that can be useful: Roll a single hair strand between the tips of your thumb and index finger. You have fine hair if you can hardly feel it or see it.

In general, it's a good idea to stay away from shampoos that contain sulfates and silicone, regardless of the type of hair you have. These components may make your shampoo foam up and leave your hair feeling clean, but over time, they may dry out your hair. If you have fine, dry, or frizzy hair, this is especially true for you.

When styling your hair, there are a few things you can do, from straightening to curling and everything in between.

If you're hoping to **straighten your hair,** you can try one of two common methods, depending on your time, your tools, and how your hair responds.

Using a Straightening Iron:

- Wash and blow dry your hair
- Use heat protection spray
- Divide your hair into sections
- Choose the right temperature for your hair on your straightening iron
- Straighten with slow movements

- Once you've straightened all your hair, use a finishing product

Straightening with a Hair Dryer:

- Wash your hair using products designed for your hair type
- Comb your hair out while conditioning
- Towel dry your hair until damp
- Using a t-shirt or scarf instead of a towel will help decrease frizz
- Use a wide-toothed comb to remove any tangles
- Add a straightening serum or cream
- Use a heat protectant
- Pick a good hair dryer to dry your hair
- You can add an attachment that streamlines the air
- Dry your hair with the strands blowing down
- Divide your hair into sections
- Blow dry the undersides
- Aim the nozzle of your hair dryer down while you brush through it
- Using a round brush will help add volume at the roots
- End with the cool setting

MAKEUP 101

One of the best ways to learn how to put on makeup is to watch free videos online. There are several influencers you can watch with great tips.

There's some makeup you might choose to wear each day, while other products you may keep for special occasions. A few examples of common makeup products are listed below.

- Primer
- Concealer
- Foundation
- Mascara
- Eyeliner
- Lipstick
- Eyeshadow

Do some research and figure out which products are best for your skin and which products fit your budget with good reviews. When choosing makeup, don't go for the cheapest brand.

You can often find palettes of colors that not only go together but match your skin shade as well. You can tell whether your skin might work well with cooler or warmer tones by looking at the thin skin on the inside of your wrist. If your veins appear blue, your skin is cool-toned. If the veins are greener, you are warm-toned. Knowing which tones complement your skin can help you choose the right color palettes.

Cool Shades Include:

- Green
- Blue
- Purple
- Pink

Warm Shades Include:

- Red
- Orange
- Yellow
- Green

Although this is not a hard rule, it can help you find which colors look best on you. The undertones of a color are important. For example, someone with cool-toned skin can still wear red lipstick, but it is recommended to choose a shade with purple undertones rather than a flat red.

It's essential to wash your face day and night and use the right moisturizer for your skin. Even on days you don't wear makeup, wash your face before going to bed. This will help prevent blackheads and other forms of acne as well as aid in evening out your skin tone. Moisturizers will help prevent aging and fine lines over time, and it is never too early to get into the practice of a skin care routine in the morning and at night. A good rule of thumb is to use a scrub (even if it is just olive or coconut oil mixed with coffee grounds or sugar) three times a week and a cleanser daily.

As a teen, you have a higher risk of skin blemishes such as acne. Following these tips can help you through this time.

Use over-the-counter acne treatments and wash troublesome areas twice daily with a mild cleanser.

Be on the lookout for treatments with topical benzoyl peroxide as the major active component. A cleanser should be applied with the fingertips, followed by rinsing with lukewarm water.

Apply a topical treatment containing adapalene after cleansing the skin. Adapalene can cleanse pores and stop fresh breakouts from occurring. Apply a pea-sized amount to the entire face, avoiding the mouth and eyes, which are prone to irritation. If necessary, it can also be used on the back and chest.

Refrain from using excessive amounts of face scrubs, astringents, and cleanser masks. This may aggravate acne by irritating the skin.

Don't forget to use acne medication if it is prescribed to you by a doctor or dermatologist.

Avoid touching or picking at trouble spots. This may result in infections, acne, and scars. It's a good practice to avoid touching your face altogether as this can prevent you from getting sick as well as keep your pores clear of unnecessary oils.

If you're wearing a face mask or veil, wear a clean one every day. A dirty face mask will undermine other preventative measures. Before using a mask for the first time, make sure to wash it. Cloth face masks should be washed in hot water with standard laundry detergent.

After engaging in activities that produce perspiration and oil, take a shower. Wearing a hat or headband while exercising might increase sweat and oil production.

Prevent acne with early treatment. An outbreak is more difficult to treat than a few pimples. Additionally, early therapy can lessen scarring and help avoid adult acne.

Guard skin against the sun. Acne can get worse in the sun, and some acne treatments make skin more sensitive to the sun's rays. Apply a moisturizer with sunscreen if you intend to spend time in the sun.

Avoid using too many cosmetics. Cosmetics have the potential to aggravate acne by clogging pores.

Shield skin from objects that push or cause friction. Examples could be your cell phone, your hands, your mask, or anything else that touches your face on a regular basis.

Be mindful of your stress levels. Acne might worsen as a result of stress.

Pay attention to your diet. A healthy diet may help you have healthier skin.

Make an appointment with a dermatologist or your doctor if your acne doesn't seem to be getting any better, despite following all these tips.

THE IMPORTANCE
OF SUNSCREEN

The earlier you start using sunscreen regularly, the more probable it is that you'll keep your collagen levels higher as you get older. Additionally, this helps to avoid cumulative damage. Don't wait until you're older to begin using a sunscreen every day. Choose a broad-spectrum sunscreen with an SPF of 15 or higher after moisturizing, and follow the application instructions.

SHAVING

Shaving can be a pain in the side, but there are ways to make the task less of a chore. And following these tips may help you get a closer shave.

The first tip, and possibly the most important, is to never dry shave. Dry shaving increases the possibility of nicks or irritation. In order to get a close shave, whatever part of your body you're about to shave should soak for at least ten minutes in warm water to soften. Then, take the time to exfoliate.

Once the warm water softens your skin, you'll want to switch to cooler water. When shaving, use shaving cream and not soap. It's important to pay attention to which way your hair is growing. For a closer shave, work against the growth of the hair.

After you've hit all the spots you plan to shave, turn the water back to warm for a bit to close your pores. Don't forget to put lotion on your skin after you shave.

FEMININE MEDICAL APPOINTMENTS

Up to the age of seventeen, you should have an annual "well-child visit" with a physician or nurse. Talk with your doctor about any questions you have about your health.

Typically, teens should first see a gynecologist between the ages of thirteen and fifteen.

The majority of the time, your first session is an opportunity to introduce yourself to the gynecologist and build a rapport. You might be anxious about this visit. That's normal. Take your time and ask whatever questions you have before the exam.

The HPV vaccine will be a significant subject during your initial patient consultations. Most cervical cancers have a sexually transmitted infection as a risk factor.

The HPV vaccine, which requires two or three doses and is best administered at age eleven or twelve, is one of the most effective preventative measures, according to doctors.

In general, you will only see the gynecologist once a year. It's important to find one that you feel comfortable with, as this is a doctor you will continue to see throughout your life. If you're not sure who you should see, talk with friends and family to see who they suggest.

FEMININE HYGIENE PRODUCTS

One of the biggest choices you make regarding feminine hygiene products is whether you will use tampons or feminine napkins, also known as pads, or a reusable product such as absorbent underwear or a menstrual cup.

Each choice has advantages and disadvantages, so it's a good idea to try multiple products before deciding which is best for you. Additionally, depending on your daily activities, you might discover that you want to alternate between products.

Pads are the most commonly used products, especially for younger women. They are a strip of disposable cloth used to line the inside of your underwear. There are different thicknesses available depending on your flow. Thin panty liners are also a type of pad, but they are usually used to help protect underwear from possible leakage while using a tampon or when there is risk of spotting (bleeding small amounts between periods). Although pads are usually more comfortable than tampons, some women find them bulky and keeping them in place can provide a challenge during intense sports.

Tampons usually come with a plastic or cardboard application tube which allows you to insert an absorbent cotton strip inside yourself. Most women prefer to use tampons if they are active or plan on swimming. They are more discreet than pads, but they also come with a couple of setbacks. For example, tampons should be changed frequently as keeping them in too long can cause toxic shock syndrome. They are also prone to leaking, which is why they are usually used with a panty liner or absorbent underwear. As they are inserted inside of you, they can also be uncomfortable. Every woman is shaped differently, and this is part of the reason tampons are not always the best choice.

Absorbent underwear is a great option that has only been available in the last few years. Unlike pads and tampons, it is reusable which makes for an environmentally friendly option. These will cost about three times as much as regular underwear but will last for years if properly cared for, which makes them an economic option compared to pads and tampons. Although this is a less bulky option than pads, there will still be panty lines, which some women do not like. If your flow is heavy, you can still use these, but they will need to be changed more frequently than if you have a lighter flow. Most brands can be washed like normal underwear; however, it is recommended to soak them in cold water to rinse out some of the blood. You can do this easily by soaking them in the bathroom sink while you shower. For an extra layer of cleanliness, you can store the dirty ones in a mesh laundry bag to keep them separate from the rest of your laundry.

Menstrual cups are another reusable option. If absorbent underwear are the eco-friendly version of pads, then menstrual cups are the tampon equivalent. These are nice because they can be used while swimming. Menstrual cups are small, flexible cups that are inserted like a tampon. Where these are discreet, they can be messy when they are removed; however, most women have no issue once they've had enough practice. To clean, you simply remove the cup, dump the blood into the toilet, and then wash the cup in the sink. One thing that's nice about this option is that these can be stored in a small bag which can be easily kept on hand.

When choosing what you want to use, it's important to consider your lifestyle. Do you love to be in the water, or are you active in sports or working out? You might choose to use a combination of options depending on what you have planned and what feels most comfortable.

The time you should truly consider wearing a pad or absorbent underwear is when you're sleeping. This is especially important if you're sleeping the recommended seven to nine hours of sleep. Tampons should be changed every four to six hours to prevent bacteria from building up and causing toxic shock syndrome.

Of course, your flow may dictate what your options are. If you notice clotting during your period, talk with your gynecologist to find out how much is normal and how much might be a concern.

Getting used to your menstruation cycle can be a little overwhelming at first, but once you get the hang of it, you can alleviate the anxiety surrounding it.

Typically, one cycle is around twenty-eight days and bleeding lasts anywhere from a couple of days to a week. You may find that you are more irritable during the days before and after your period. You might also feel bloated or have menstrual cramps. Talk with your doctor if any of these issues start to influence your everyday life or if your cycles don't seem to follow the normal twenty-eight-day pattern.

EMOTIONAL AND MENTAL HEALTH ON YOUR PERIOD

One thing that is often neglected is mental health during this time. Hormonal fluctuations are completely normal and affect every woman differently. Sometimes the symptoms can be extreme in the week before your period.

It's not a bad idea to keep a mood journal—even if it's just a couple words jotted in the notes on your phone. There are many period apps designed to help you track your cycles. This can be helpful because you can record your moods in the app to help track your natural pattern. It's not uncommon for doctors to prescribe small doses of fast-acting mood stabilizers to temper more extreme fluctuations.

Although it is vital to remember that mood fluctuations are normal, you should pay special attention to increased anxiety, depression, or suicidal thoughts preceding your period. If you experience any of these, talk to your doctor and trusted adults so they can help you decide the best course of action. Regardless of what decision you make, increasing self-care, practicing strengthening emotional tolerance, and finding healthy coping strategies should be implemented. Below are some ideas.

Self-Care:

Exercise can help soothe intense emotions and anxiety by creating an energetic outlet. It also releases endorphins, which will help boost your mood. If running or strength training is not your thing, that's okay! Dancing like a loon in your room to your favorite music, taking a long walk somewhere pretty, or sledding with a best friend are all examples of mood-lifting physical activities.

Take a bath. Warm water therapy is a great way to soothe your muscles and mind. The bathtub is a good place for emotional catharsis. Before you get started, make sure you give your household a heads up and give them a chance to use the bathroom. If you don't have a tub at your house, ask a friend's parents if you can use theirs. Most women get it and will help you if you let them know what you need.

This is your time, so make it extra special. If you're not making your own money yet, you may have to get creative, but even if you can only get hot water around your feet, you can still make this a relaxing venture. Before your bath, gather whatever you can to pamper yourself. Bath bombs, bubble bath, Epsom salt, candles, essential oils, face scrubs or masks, good music, audio books, paperback books you don't mind getting wet, coffee, or tea are all great ideas. You can make your own face scrubs and masks out of all kinds of common staples like coffee, sugar, bananas, rice water, or tomato juice. In addition to the warm water helping soothe your body and mind, this is also a good place to just let it all out. If you need to cry, cry all you want. The bathtub is also a great place to practice meditation—just make sure not to fall asleep!

Get cozy. If you are feeling overwhelmed about work and school and life, take a moment. Put on the most comfortable outfit you own, pour yourself a hot cup of tea, and binge watch your favorite show.

This self-care practice can be very helpful, as long as you're careful that it doesn't become a form of procrastination. If you are tempted to do this instead of a task you're trying to avoid, set a timer for twenty minutes and bust out as much of that task as you can first. More often than not, you'll find yourself finishing the task completely which will boost your self-esteem, lower your anxiety, and make snuggling up all the more rewarding.

CHAPTER FOUR:
LET'S TALK ABOUT MENTAL HEALTH

Mental health is a serious concern at any age. Unfortunately, we don't always pay attention to it until it's too late. Keep reading to learn some things you should understand about depression, such as when to get help and more.

Paying attention to how you feel and how your friends are behaving is essential. It may feel wrong to seek help for a friend, but sometimes depression is hard to pinpoint and we need help from others. In the same way, don't be upset with a friend who might worry about you.

We need to work toward a point where mental health isn't thought of as a taboo subject and we can support our friends and family who struggle at times. After all, letting them know we care and want them around for a long time shouldn't be a bad thing.

WHAT IS NORMAL?

It's totally normal for teenagers (and adults) to feel occasional sadness or rage. It's not typical for these bad feelings to last for several days or even weeks. In some circumstances, experiencing sadness or grief over an extended period of time can be normal. For example, if a family member has passed away, including a pet, or if your family is going through a traumatic event (like losing your home), experiencing sadness over an extended period of time may simply be a necessary part of working through the stages of grief. However, if you or a friend appear to be angry or depressed for an extended length of time without apparent cause, it may be a sign of depression.

CHANGES IN HOW YOU FEEL PHYSICALLY

Many people are unaware that physical pain can often accompany depression. If you or a friend frequently complains of headaches, stomachaches, or other aches and pains all over their body, the explanation may not be physical at all. There could be a chemical imbalance rather than a physical ailment that is the root of the problem.

CHANGES IN EATING

Teenagers frequently eat in response to their emotions, much like adults. Depression may be to blame if you or a friend suddenly lose all appetite and appear to be losing weight or eating more than normal and gaining weight.

CHANGES IN ACTIVITY

Teenagers who are depressed may lose interest in past favorite activities. It's common for young people to explore new things and occasionally give up on their previous hobbies and sports. However, this could indicate depression if someone isn't taking up new hobbies to replace those they're no longer interested in.

The same is true of quitting all your favorite activities at once. Someone who chooses to stop participating in many activities like playing soccer, volunteering at an animal shelter, and going to the beach with friends on the weekends may be exhibiting signs of depression. But a teen who decides to quit soccer and join the chess club instead is probably just trying out new things, which is typical behavior for this age group.

USING ALCOHOL OR DRUGS

While many people see alcohol or drug abuse as a separate problem from depression (and sometimes it is), the two can go together. Some teens will attempt to self-medicate their bad feelings by turning to substances, and use can quickly turn to abuse. This, in turn, can worsen depression because it can make a teen feel guilty and overwhelmed about keeping such a serious secret.

Substance abuse can also prevent you from developing the normal coping mechanisms needed to deal with emotional and physical discomforts. This time of your life can be difficult, but learning to deal with life stress and discomfort now is essential to handling these things well in adulthood.

Using drugs and alcohol to cope will increase your chances of developing dependency and life-altering addictions that can be near impossible to reverse once they take root. If a friend tells you they're worried about how you're acting, or if you're worried about a friend, talk with someone you trust.

This subject can be especially difficult since you may be admitting to drinking or using drugs as well, which can get you in trouble. It doesn't often seem like it but getting in trouble is better than possibly losing a friend, or worse, your life. Aside from the mental and physical repercussions of using these substances, you can also put yourself in extreme danger in the process of seeking out or looking for somewhere to use these substances. Most teenage bodies are not developed enough to cope with the damage caused by drugs and alcohol. Beyond that, being impaired can lead to making all kinds of decisions which put your physical, sexual, and emotional safety at risk. Protect yourself and your friends by taking this seriously.

Alcohol and drug use is often romanticized in American media, but if you are ever curious about the truth, attend an Alcoholics Anonymous or Narcotics Anonymous meeting and ask the people there what they were like when they were a teenager. You'll be surprised how many people were just like you and just like anyone you might look up to that is romanticizing partying. Seeing how casual use can easily snowball out of control can really put things into perspective. AA and NA are great resources for anyone of any age. These meetings are inviting and safe places that will keep your identity and story secret. You can find them in almost every town as well as online on Zoom.

HOW ARE
YOU SLEEPING?

If given the option, many teenagers would choose to stay up late and sleep in. It's nice to engage in this conduct on the weekends and during vacations, which is entirely normal behavior. However, if your sleep patterns are bothering you or interfering with your hobbies and academics, there might be something more to your sleeping pattern. This mental health issue may result in insomnia or sleeping even longer than is usually necessary. Teenagers with depression occasionally swing back and forth between the two extremes.

If you find yourself missing activities with friends, choosing to sleep your days away, or not sleeping at all, find someone to talk to. Several things might play into your sleep patterns, so it's good to narrow down what is happening.

SLIP IN GRADES OR
SOCIALIZATION AT SCHOOL

If you or a friend has a substantial dip in academic performance, it could indicate a more serious issue. That "something serious" might occasionally be sadness, loneliness, burnout, or another type of mental health ailment. Depression has a tendency to drain a person's motivation, which is one reason why it can result in bad grades. If you've always been driven to maintain good grades, excel in extracurricular activities, or hold down a job, the disappearance of this drive merits investigation.

Keep in mind that depression and anxiety can be associated with current circumstances like how life is going at home, whether or not you are on good terms with your friends, or if something bad or traumatic has recently happened in your life. In past generations mental health was not understood and was often stigmatized, discouraging people from seeking help. Many people considered it a lifetime diagnosis if the word depression or anxiety was associated with them. This isn't always the case, though, which is why you shouldn't hesitate to seek out someone professional to talk to.

There are so many temporary circumstances that can trigger a fluctuation in mental health. Some examples might be discovering your best friend betraying you, fearing you are unpopular, fearing failure when it comes to graduating, experiencing performance anxiety regarding exams or major life changes, experiencing traumatic events such as a car accident, the death of a loved one, or the divorce of your parents. If you have an alcoholic parent or a toxic environment at home, this can make you feel unbalanced, insecure, or unstable. Maybe your family is perfectly normal, but you are just different from them—feeling alienated, misunderstood, or not accepted can really impact your mental health. Luckily there are now many options available to you, including online services such as BetterHelp, which provide professional help at lower costs and with easier access.

HOW DO YOU GET
THE HELP YOU NEED?

Everyone needs a support system, especially when it feels like you don't want anyone near you or your personal life. That may sound strange, but sometimes when you least want support, that's when you need it the most.

What comes to your mind when you hear the word "support"? Are you able to envision something? Do you have any tense areas of your body? What terms or definitions spring to mind? What else have you observed? Take some time to reflect, either in your head or in writing, as you see fit.

Support can be anything that helps you feel better, as long as the support is healthy for you. Anything that inspires or strengthens you counts. Keep in mind that everyone needs support as they travel through life, and depending on the day, their mood, the circumstance, etc., most people will need to draw from a variety of sources. A support system is important for everyone!

WHAT AND WHO MAKE UP YOUR SUPPORT SYSTEM?

Yes, you can receive support from both people and things. It's up to you what or who gives you support.

What can you offer or do to comfort yourself when you are upset or stressed? Think about your five senses and possible actions and gestures. Giving yourself a hug, rubbing your shoulders, going for a run, snuggling in bed, or spending some time journaling are a few things on my list.

Family or Friends: Who can you call or text for support when you're anxious, depressed, or overwhelmed? Who can you turn to for assistance? List the names of the relatives and friends you feel most at ease contacting in times of need and enthusiasm.

Professionals: Who in your life do you consider to be "professionals" who support you? Consider the grownups you encounter in your neighborhood and school. I seek help from my acupuncturist, my writing group, other coaches, authors (even if only through their books), and therapists.

Places: Where do you feel free, happy, safe, and secure? Think about the areas within and outside your house, close by and far away, actual and imagined. For instance, you can have a fantasy location that you've only ever been to in your imagination, and you might also adore spending time in a particular area of the public library.

Surroundings: What modifications to your environment do you find soothing and comforting? Think about your five senses once more. Take note of your favorite tastes, textures, noises, smells, and other senses.

Other Supports: Lastly, consider anything (or anyone) else that you feel affirmed and supported by. These can be quotes, lyrics, foods, or activities.

Next, keep in mind that you need to employ your support network for this to work. When you need it, it's there for you, but you'll need a trigger or cue to use it. Select a method for contacting your support network. Then, after a week or so, pay attention to how frequently you use it. From there, make adjustments and choose where you want to store the information (your screen saver or on your bathroom mirror, for example).

Where could you save this knowledge so you can access it when needed? Is it digital or printed? In a list or presented in the form of sketches or doodles?

Support is key. You will need support systems for the rest of your life. It's important to understand that these support systems will change over time, and there may be times when you have to drop someone from your support system if you find they don't have your best interests in mind. Our support systems also change when we change. Throughout your life, you will go through significant stages that will require you to be flexible and open-minded about who you lean on.

THE POWER OF POSITIVE
TALK AND AFFIRMATIONS

Let's brainstorm all the emotions you've ever had. This is just for fun but take a few minutes to think about it.

What's on your list? Most likely, you listed emotions like joy, sorrow, excitement, anger, fear, gratitude, pride, confusion, stress, relaxation, and amazement.

Now, divide your list of feelings into two groups: positive and negative emotions.

Being able to experience both pleasant and negative emotions comes naturally to us. Even while we may refer to more challenging emotions as "negative," this does not imply that they are undesirable or that we shouldn't feel them. However, the majority of people undoubtedly prefer to experience happy emotions rather than negative ones. You probably prefer to be joyful rather than depressed and confident rather than unsure.

What counts is how well-balanced our emotions are—how much of each kind of emotion, whether pleasant or negative, we feel.

CAN NEGATIVE EMOTIONS HELP YOU?

Negative emotions alert us to potential dangers or difficulties that we may have to face. For instance, fear can warn us of potential danger. It serves as a warning that we might need to defend ourselves. Anger alerts us to someone treading on our toes, going over the line, or betraying our trust. Anger may be an indication that we need to defend our own interests.

Our consciousness is focused on negative emotions. They often assist us in focusing on a problem so that we can address it. However, experiencing too many unfavorable feelings might leave us feeling overburdened, nervous, worn out, or pressured. Problems may feel insurmountable when negative emotions are out of balance.

HOW DO POSITIVE EMOTIONS HELP US?

Positive emotions counterbalance negative ones, but they also have other potent advantages.

Positive emotions alter our brains in ways that broaden our awareness, attention, and memory instead of narrowing them, as negative emotions do. They enable us to process more information, hold multiple thoughts simultaneously, and comprehend how various ideas are related to one another.

Positive emotions help us see new possibilities, which makes it easier for us to learn new things and advance our talents. As a result, you perform better on assignments and assessments.

People who regularly experience positive emotions have a tendency to be happier, healthier, more intelligent, and socially adept.

WHAT TO DO IF YOU NEED HELP OUTSIDE YOUR SUPPORT SYSTEM?

All teenagers experience problems, from mood swings to academic difficulties. However, there are situations when your distress may reach a point where you should seek professional assistance.

Therapy doesn't necessarily have to be saved for significant mental health issues or life-altering occurrences. Meeting with a therapist helps stop minor problems from developing into bigger ones. Consider mental health treatment to be like sunscreen. You put it on to protect yourself from sunburn. If you ever find yourself in a predicament you don't know how to get out of, speaking with a professional can be helpful.

Ask a dependable friend or member of your family if they think you would benefit from speaking with a mental health professional. You don't need to be concerned about attending multiple sessions or having anxiety before speaking. Sometimes a significant improvement can be seen after just a few therapy sessions. Additionally, your therapist will allow you to disclose as little or as much as you like. Just keep in mind that what you receive out of anything depends on how much you put into it.

There is so much to gain from visiting with a therapist to discuss a range of issues, from doubts about what you want to do with your future to problems in your relationships.

Some common reasons your peers might go to therapy are discussed further below. You do not have to be dealing with one of these issues to set up a session. Just knowing you need to talk with someone is all you need.

Depression: Mood disorders frequently begin in adolescence. Depression can persist throughout adulthood if untreated. The foundation of successful treatment is a precise diagnosis and early intervention. Don't be embarrassed or worried. Depression affects a wide number of people, but things can get better.

Anxiety: Teenagers occasionally worry, which is common, but some also experience severe anxiety. Academics and friendships are only two of the many things in your life that might cause anxiety. This goes beyond normal worry. Anxiety can keep you up at night or cause you to eat too much or too little. If you're worried about your worry, and it's affecting your life, talk to someone.

Substance Abuse Issues: Teenagers, unfortunately, can develop major issues with drugs and alcohol. If you are experimenting with substances, you are at risk of not only addiction but harming yourself and others.

Stress: Teenagers are susceptible to stress. Stress can have a negative impact, whether it comes from the pressure to perform well on a test or worries about what to do after high school. Teens who receive therapy can develop effective coping mechanisms for stress, which will benefit them throughout their lives.

When your stress becomes too big for you to handle, it can damage relationships with friends and family.

Issues with Self-Esteem: While most teenagers encounter self-confidence issues at some point, some have severe self-esteem problems. Teenagers are more likely to experience difficulties like substance misuse and academic failure when these issues are not addressed.

Your self-esteem can be strengthened with the help of therapy. Instead of feeling like no one understands you or feels the way you do, you'll find out through therapy that your thoughts aren't necessarily true. There are plenty of teens and adults who feel the same way you do. Your therapist might even suggest a support system. If they do, consider going. It might be the best choice you make.

Grief: The loss of a loved one can be particularly tough throughout adolescence because teens process grief in a different way than adults do. You can benefit from individual, family, or group therapy to sort out your emotions and make sense of your loss.

You might be reading this and thinking that there is no way you're going to sit in a room with a stranger and talk about what's bothering you. Many people feel the same way when first approached with the idea of therapy. There are many different options, though. Before deciding it's "never going to happen," try a session or research what options are available for you.

Remote Therapy

In our remote world, you might even be able to attend therapy from your bedroom. With online options available, access to therapy services has increased a great deal in just the last two years. With most services, you can look through a list of therapists before deciding which one will work for you.

For instance, you may know you only want to speak to a female therapist, and maybe you want that therapist to be younger. You can look for those parameters when narrowing down who you want to see.

WHAT IS CBT?

One of the most common types of therapy for teens is Cognitive Behavioral Therapy (CBT).

Making connections between thoughts, behaviors, and feelings is a key component of Cognitive Behavioral Therapy. CBT-trained therapists assist clients in recognizing and altering problematic patterns.

For teens, CBT can help with numerous conditions, such as eating disorders, substance abuse, anxiety, and depression.

The foundation of CBT is the idea that there is a direct connection between thoughts, behaviors, and feelings. For instance, if you believe you are socially uncomfortable, you will feel anxious and avoid social situations. CBT teaches you to recognize your unhelpful, habitual thoughts and replace them with realistic, useful ones.

How Does CBT Help?

Teenagers frequently have distorted core self-beliefs. CBT aids in addressing and correcting these distortions. A therapist utilizing CBT would assist a teen in recognizing the negative thought patterns that contribute to mental health issues.

To help detect disordered thoughts, a therapist may provide a series of questions and request that you keep a thought journal. This helps to track the patterns of your thoughts so you and the therapist can talk about how to decrease or even stop those thoughts.

Advantages of CBT

CBT teaches teenagers how to perceive their world in new ways. CBT is typically a short-term therapy compared to other therapeutic options.

The strategy also deals with challenges in the present because it is heavily problem focused. It's unlikely your therapist will talk to you about when you were younger or try to interpret your behavior in a deeper way. Instead, sessions concentrate on assisting you with current issues.

What Benefits Does CBT Have?

- Modifies unproductive mental processes
- Improves interpersonal communication
- Recognizes healthy responses to stress
- Helps to stop thoughts that make you act in ways that are destructive or addictive
- Reduces phobias and fears

HOW CAN YOU PREPARE
FOR THERAPY?

Your therapist will work with you to gain new perspectives and coping mechanisms.

They may give you "homework" to complete outside of therapy sessions, which may entail honing many of the skills you are learning. CBT is frequently very structured, which might be advantageous for you, especially if you want to progress through therapy quickly. In order to change your way of thinking, though, you'll have to open up and do the homework.

OTHER TYPES
OF THERAPY

Family Therapy

In some instances, family therapy might be beneficial to work through what is going on in your life. If this worries you, do not let it stop you from attending your individual sessions. Your therapist will work with you in determining when and if family therapy is necessary.

Alternative Therapy Types

Alternative modes of healing are beneficial since they provide you with a selection to try if the conventional paths of healing don't work. It may also help you see how the body and mind can heal themselves in ways that go beyond the scope of conventional treatment.

Now, it should be emphasized that while some of the methods listed below are becoming more and more popular, others have not been shown to be effective.

As a result, the list of alternative healing options provided below can support your existing healing process rather than urging you to abandon the ones you're presently using. Essentially, you can add these alongside your therapy sessions with your therapist.

Additionally, you might discover the healing techniques below in an increasing number of locations, like hospitals or teen residential treatment centers. When you need options, being aware of these choices can help:

Acupuncture is an alternative medical practice that includes inserting needles into the body's tissues or skin in order to cure a variety of mental, emotional, and physical ailments as well as to relieve pain.

Essential oils from plants and herbs are used in **aromatherapy**; they can be applied topically or inhaled. Natural plant-based aromas have been demonstrated to assist emotional balance, stress alleviation, and general well-being.

Images from your imagination are used in **art therapy**. These images may occasionally be self-destructive when the mind is afflicted by sickness, resulting in teen addiction, depression, and suicide.

It might be challenging to feel deserving of everything life has to give you, for instance, if you hold an ashamed, unworthy, or unlovable view of yourself. Finding the strength to deal with the emotional, psychological, and physical changes that occur during adolescence may be challenging.

Through the use of focus and imagination, **guided imagery** is a form of therapy that concentrates on the neurological system, especially the area of the body that may contain the solution to a patient's problem. It can be applied to people who suffer from addiction and other dual-diagnosis conditions.

Herbs are organic botanical substances that have a therapeutic effect on the body, and they are used in **herbal therapy**. Herbs have been utilized for cleansing for a very long time. This type of therapy might be used in conjunction with aromatherapy.

Equine therapy is quite popular for teens as it allows you to connect with animals in nature. You do not need to have your own horse. You can find someone trained in equine therapy online.

The options that are possible for you depend on where you live and what you have access to. The first step, once you decide you need help, is to talk with someone. It might be a counselor at school, a coach, or a parent. Most of these options will require permission from a guardian.

What about Confidentiality?

Just because you need permission to receive therapy in most instances doesn't mean that your parent is allowed to know everything that is said during your sessions. There are ground rules that your therapist will talk with you about.

Confidentiality is a crucial element of therapy and contributes significantly to its effectiveness.

If teens thought that the information they provided in counseling sessions would be shared with others after the fact, they would be less likely to seek counseling. Even attending a group session in a less private setting might make you less likely to express the emotions and issues that are necessary for therapy to be effective.

As a result, licensed mental health professionals like psychologists, counselors, therapists, and social workers adhere to ethical standards that prevent clients' identities and conversations from being revealed outside of therapy without the client's written consent, or "informed consent," which is a term used to describe this practice.

What Does That Mean?

There are various limits to client-therapist confidentiality that impact clients of all ages and other gray areas specific to teen counseling and therapy.

If a client discloses child, elderly, or disabled person abuse, the therapist must report it.

Counselors and therapists must disclose threats to personal safety, including clients' intentions to hurt themselves or others.

Teen counselors and therapists should always discuss confidentiality issues with kids and parents before treatment begins.

A teen's faith in his or her therapist is crucial to the success of counseling and therapy. You must trust your therapist to keep what is shared confidential. If you don't, you won't feel comfortable sharing much.

Due to the uniqueness of each child and the issues they experience, as well as local, state, and national laws regulating confidentiality and disclosure, therapists, teens, and their parents often agree on different confidentiality arrangements.

You and your therapist might come up with alternate options, such as a compromise about parent engagement. Your therapist might ask you to provide your parents with regular updates on the issues being worked on in treatment and progress. This is often enough for your loved ones to feel comfortable in the situation. Additionally, your therapist should inform you if they have to disclose something you've discussed.

Teens, parents, and therapists should discuss confidentiality and informed permission before therapy begins. You should feel free to ask questions about privacy, confidentiality, and any other concerns you have.

MEDITATION AND MINDFULNESS

In discussing alternative therapeutic options above, guided imagery was introduced. We'll take a more detailed look at this, as well as mindfulness and meditation. All three options are great for keeping your stress at bay as you navigate your teen years.

Anyone can benefit greatly from meditation, and as you grow older you will appreciate your ability to fully focus on the present and disengage from thoughts about everything else. This is essential when it feels like your thoughts are caving in on you.

Over the age of nine, people become more aware of their ideas, and we may start exploring meditations that include changing our thoughts or putting our thoughts aside and going deep within.

Here are a few meditations provided by doyou.com that can be especially helpful for pre-teens and teens:

Thought Hunter

Close your eyes and remain motionless while counting slowly from one to ten. If you have any interrupting thoughts, simply return to counting from one.

Keep an eye out for even the smallest thought. Since this is a practice of honesty between you and yourself, you must return to counting from one at the first sign of even the smallest thought, sound, or idea.

This activity teaches us to become more conscious of our thoughts. Unconscious ideas are the ones that cause us to feel the way we feel, want the things we want, and do actions that we may not have taken with more conscious consideration.

Being conscious of those fleeting, quiet thoughts is the first step toward being able to change them and alter the course of our lives. It doesn't take more than a minute or two to complete this workout.

Counting Meditation

Count slowly in your head from one hundred down to one while seated or lying on your back. Counting backward demands more concentration and will help you maintain your focus.

Stay with the numbers and try not to worry about anything else. Restart your count at one hundred if you lose track. If you get to one, continue to be silent for a little while longer.

This is a fantastic exercise for improving focus, and if you can keep your attention on the task at hand long enough to reach one without getting sidetracked, you will have a stunning and very calming inner experience. Test it out for yourself!

Breath Meditation

Close your eyes and sit up straight. Start taking deep breaths until you can hear your breath. As you breathe in and out, pay attention to how your body feels as the air passes through your nose. Try to feel how the air contacts your top lip or how it makes contact with the inside of your nose.

Now, progressively soften the breath and let it flow naturally while continuing to pay attention to its sound.

Try to focus just on your breath and ignore your thoughts.

Refocus on your breath whenever you start to think about something else.

The same meditation can be performed similarly by paying close attention to your heartbeat and listening to it.

Additionally, there are meditations available on YouTube and on applications like Calm and Headspace. Even five minutes a day of meditation can have a profound impact.

Things to Remember for Your Mental Health

Asking for assistance while coping with a mental health issue is a sign of strength for teenagers who are struggling.

To acknowledge that you might not be able to face your issues alone requires a lot of courage and work. Teenagers sometimes hesitate to speak their minds, thinking they're being bothersome.

They often worry that, because they can't handle things themselves, someone will think they failed. This couldn't be further from the truth. If you are talking to someone and they make you feel that way, find someone else to talk to.

Maintaining a healthy lifestyle will help you maintain mental equilibrium.

Everything changes quickly during adolescence. You're growing and changing all the time. You are developing and moving toward more independence, which makes choosing healthy options even more important.

You need to eat well, sleep well, and talk kindly to yourself. You also need to reach out when necessary and stay physically active.

Following a schedule or routine can be a good approach to maintaining mental balance when coping with stressful issues. Keeping yourself busy will keep your thoughts away from the bad things in your life.

Teen minds sorely need the sensation of accomplishment that comes with achieving goals.

Want to know a secret? Adult minds work the same way. If you can learn some of these coping skills as a teen, you'll be unstoppable as an adult!

Things to Remind Yourself Each Day

- My life is in my hands
- I'm intelligent
- I am different
- I have a goal
- I am fabulous

The easiest way to remember your strength is to tell yourself these affirmations every day.

We all have really admirable traits. They must not be forgotten. They should serve as continual reminders that obstacles can be surmounted and successful outcomes are conceivable.

Coping mechanisms for managing mental health come in a wide variety. Problems with mental health can be handled. There are numerous paths you can follow to learn how to maintain your mental health. We've only introduced a few in this book.

SURROUND YOURSELF
WITH POSITIVITY

You'll recover more quickly if you surround yourself with positive influences. It is far more difficult to manage a mental health issue when bullying and dysfunctional relationships are present.

Finding friends who encourage you and are kind to you can help you maintain positivity in your life.

Many of the negative effects of having a mental health problem are alleviated by talking about it. Perhaps talk more about support, support groups, and family support. Be careful not to generalize or assert that receiving help alone makes dealing with a mental health issue any easier.

CHAPTER FIVE:
PHYSICAL HEALTH

Exercise can play a significant role in preserving your health as a teenager. Maintaining a healthy lifestyle now will help you immensely when you get older.

CREATE A WORKOUT SCHEDULE

A regular exercise schedule is an enjoyable way to create heart-healthy behaviors and spend time moving with loved ones. The suggestions for teen fitness provided below can help you plan activities for yourself.

Teenagers should focus on exercising for at least sixty minutes of moderate to vigorous intensity each day to maintain a healthy weight during growth. Aerobic exercise is necessary to build bones and muscles.

Exercise that is low- to moderate-intensity for even thirty minutes a day is good. The secret is to move every day. Examples of these activities include the following:

- Dancing
- Workout videos at home
- Running
- Swimming
- Cycling
- Gymnastics
- Hiking
- Soccer

Teenagers who engage in regular exercise may be able to prevent conditions such as weight gain, high blood pressure, abnormal cholesterol levels, and hazardous lifestyle decisions that could lead to a heart attack or stroke in the future.

Exercising consistently is crucial to living a healthy lifestyle. But don't go overboard. Maintain your comfort level. Speak with the school nurse or your doctor if you have concerns about your weight or level of fitness.

Your capacity for endurance grows with regular aerobic exercise. Don't forget to drink plenty of water while you're exercising to avoid dehydration. And once you're finished, continue drinking water as you recover.

ADVANTAGES OF REGULAR EXERCISE

Do you wonder what else you can get out of physical exercise? These things might not seem like a big deal right now, but they are benefits you'll appreciate as you grow older.

- Increases the body's blood flow
- Controls your weight
- Slows down the oxidative stress of the body
- Lowers and controls high blood pressure
- Stops bone loss
- Increases energy

- Reduces stress
- Enhances the capacity to sleep soundly and swiftly
- Enhances self-image
- Alleviates stress
- Fights despair and anxiety
- Increases excitement and optimism
- Increases muscular strength

EATING HEALTHY

If you're going to exercise as you should, you should also make sure to eat well. Here are several things you can do as a teenager to make sure you're eating the right things.

The teenage years are a time of incredible changes. It can be overwhelming, to say the least. It's essential to make sure you choose healthy foods consistently. Finding a good balance can be hard, especially if you're active. It can seem like you're hungry all the time! It's hard to not just give in and overindulge in unhealthy snacks that are heavy in fat, sugar, or salt.

WHAT SHOULD
YOU EAT?

Eat a nutritious, balanced diet that satisfies your energy requirements. You should focus on five primary food groups:

- Veggies and fruit
- Bread, pasta, rice, potatoes, and other starchy foods
- Proteins such as fish, eggs, beans, and pulses
- Dairy and substitutes
- Spreads and oils

Fruits and Veggies

Consumption of five servings of fruit and vegetables each day is suggested for all age groups. Five pieces a day are recommended to help prevent heart disease and some types of cancer, according to research. Fruits and vegetables are low in fat and high in vitamins, minerals, and fiber.

You should shoot for roughly 80g. Examples of portions are as follows:

- One fruit, preferably medium-sized like an apple, orange, banana, or pear
- Two little fruits, such as plums or kiwis
- One substantial slice of melon or pineapple
- One spoonful of raisins

- Three heaping teaspoons of vegetables, either fresh or frozen
- One smoothie or glass (approximately 150 ml) of fresh fruit juice

Regardless of how much you consume, dried fruit, fruit juices, and smoothies can all only be considered as one portion each day. Juices and dried fruit should both be consumed with a meal because their high sugar content may harm teeth.

Bread and Other Starchy Foods

Meals should be built around starchy foods like bread, rice, potatoes, and pasta because they are a wonderful source of energy, fiber, and B vitamins.

Choose whole-grain products that are higher in fiber, such as whole wheat pasta, brown rice, or potatoes that still have their skin on.

Compared to white or refined starchy foods, whole-grain foods typically have higher levels of other nutrients and more fiber. Additionally, because we digest whole grains more slowly, you'll feel full longer when you eat whole-grain foods.

Although the butter or creamy sauces that are frequently added to starchy dishes might increase their fat level, starchy foods themselves are low in fat.

Proteins

Because they are naturally very low in fat and high in fiber, protein, vitamins, and minerals, legumes such as beans, peas, and lentils make excellent meat substitutes.

Eggs are an easy and incredibly adaptable substitute for meat. They can be cooked, poached, scrambled, or made into omelets.

Two servings of fish each week are advised for young people. Salmon is a great option. All forms of fish—fresh, frozen, and canned—are good choices.

Iron, vitamin B12, and protein are all found in meat. Iron deficiency anemia, a prevalent illness in teenage girls, can be avoided with a diet high in iron. Limit your intake of processed meats and poultry products because they are poor in iron and rich in fat and salt.

Dairy and Dairy Substitutes

Calcium, vitamins A and D, B12, protein, and fat are all vital nutrients found in milk and dairy products (and substitutes), including yogurt and cheese. Calcium is essential for healthy neuron and muscle function as well as bone growth.

Calcium absorption requires vitamin D, which is why it is crucial for constructing strong bones.

Try to select products with less fat, like half-fat cheddar, cottage cheese, Edam cheese, and semi-skimmed or skimmed milk. Choose unsweetened, calcium-fortified dairy substitutes like almond or soy.

Spreads and Oils

Consuming adequate amounts of good fats is crucial for development and growth. Unsaturated oils and spreads like rapeseed, olive, or sunflower are the best.

You might be wondering how this list helps you, especially since someone else might do the grocery shopping for your family. That doesn't mean you can't participate, though.

Maybe you can help with meal planning for the family. You might even gain some skills by learning how to cook healthy meals. Knowing how to cook, meal plan, and budget for food is an essential skill for all teens to learn.

MAINTAINING A HEALTHY WEIGHT

You should be able to maintain a healthy weight if you are physically active and consume a healthy, balanced diet.

If you are overweight, you should consume a balanced diet, make an effort to reduce the amount of sugar and fat, and engage in lots of physical activity. Remember, get up and exercise each day to keep yourself physically fit.

It's a smart idea in particular to:

- Eat fewer cookies, cakes, and candies.
- Eat fewer processed meals, such as quick noodles, and fatty items like chips, burgers, and fried food.
- Regularly consume balanced meals.
- Base your meals on starchy foods and, whenever possible, choose whole-grain variants.
- Eat more fruit and veggies.
- Drink six to eight glasses of water or other liquids each day. (All sugar-free beverages, including tea and coffee, low-fat milk, and water, qualify).

Instead of concentrating on losing weight, it's important to prioritize eating well and staying active.

WHAT IF YOU ARE VEGAN OR VEGETARIAN?

Diets that are vegetarian or vegan can be beneficial as long as a variety of foods are consumed. You will need to take extra precautions to ensure that you get all the necessary protein, vitamins, iron, and other minerals if meat and animal products are avoided.

If you eat a vegan diet, this is especially crucial. Since riboflavin and vitamin B12 are only found in animal dietary sources, getting all the vitamins one needs while eating a vegan diet can be challenging.

Therefore, it is advised to take vitamin B12 and riboflavin (another B vitamin) supplements.

Make Sure You Are Consuming Adequate Protein

As your primary sources of protein, be careful to locate an alternative to meat, fish, and chicken. We listed some of these above, but it's important to note them again. These might consist of:

- Lentils, butter beans, kidney beans, and chickpeas (pulses)
- Legume curd (tofu)
- Bean protein (textured vegetable protein)
- Nuts, either ground or finely chopped (unless there is a family history of allergy)
- Milk, cheese, and eggs depending on your diet, but you can also find plant-based varieties.

OBTAINING ADEQUATE IRON

Teenagers, especially adolescent females who are more likely to develop iron deficiency anemia, need to consume adequate iron since it is necessary for the production of red blood cells, which transport oxygen throughout the body.

Suitable iron sources include:

- Whole-grain foods
- Green leafy foods like spinach and watercress
- Dried figs or apricots

It may be simpler to absorb iron from the diet if vitamin C-containing foods are consumed alongside foods high in iron.

Additionally, you should refrain from drinking excessive amounts of tea or coffee because they hinder the body's absorption of iron.

GETTING ENOUGH SLEEP

All age groups should prioritize getting enough sleep. All bodily systems, including the immune system, benefit from a healthy amount of sleep. Teenagers' physical health, emotional and mental growth, and academic achievement all depend on getting enough rest.

Sleep helps the brain develop and operate during adolescence, which increases attention span, memory, and cognitive skills. The physiological growth spurt that occurs throughout the teen years is supported by getting enough sleep.

It's important to know that sleep deprivation impairs academic performance by causing tiredness and a lack of attentiveness. If you don't get enough sleep, you have a higher risk of developing diabetes, hypertension, and behavioral issues in addition to depression and other mental health problems. It has been demonstrated to have a detrimental effect on sports performance as well.

You should get between eight and ten hours of sleep per night, according to the National Sleep Foundation and the American Academy of Sleep Medicine, in order to stay healthy. However, the majority of teenagers sleep for much less time each night than is advised.

This is partially a result of your circadian cycle naturally shifting, which makes it challenging for you to fall asleep before eleven o'clock. You naturally have a propensity to stay up late and sleep in more in the morning. Early start times for school, a heavy workload of homework and other schoolwork, an excessive number of extracurricular activities, a busy social life, and excessive use of technological devices are additional variables that affect your sleep.

You may stay up late to do several of these tasks or to spend time with friends on the weekends, which can all result in getting little to no sleep.

TIPS TO HELP YOU GET BETTER SLEEP

Blue light from electronics lowers melatonin production, making it harder to fall asleep. At least an hour before bed, avoid smartphones and TV. Turning off notifications on gadgets reduces distractions.

Regularize your wake-up and bedtime. Maintaining a regular sleep schedule, including weekends, is healthy. Teens who push back their bedtime on weekends have trouble returning to school sleep routines. This may cause irritability or tiredness on Mondays.

Take a warm shower, consume a hot milky drink, or do meditation or moderate yoga before bed.

Avoid caffeine, especially in the evening.

Use a supportive mattress and pillows in a cool, dark bedroom.

Stay active during the day and do at least sixty minutes of exercise per day.

BODY POSITIVITY

Women are more likely to be in good physical and mental health if they like how they look. Some mental health problems, like eating disorders and depression, are more likely to happen to girls and women who think and feel bad about their bodies. Researchers think that one reason more women than men have depression is that they are unhappy with their bodies.

A bad opinion of your body can also make you feel bad about yourself, which can affect many parts of your life. You might not want to be around other people or think about what you eat or how much you work out all the time. But you can take steps to feel better about your body.

Many events and situations from your past could make you feel bad about your body:

- Being teased or picked on because of how you looked as a child
- Being told you're ugly, too fat, too thin, or that other parts of your appearance aren't good enough (this is a form of bullying)
- Seeing things in the media or on social media that make you feel bad about the way you look
- Being underweight, overweight, or obese

The more you think positive thoughts about yourself and the less you think negative things about your body, the better you will feel about who you are and how you look. Even though few people are happy with every part of their body, focusing on the parts you do like can help. Also, as they get older, most people realize that how they look is only one part of who they are. It's better for your health to work on accepting how you look than to always try to change it.

SUPPLEMENTS
AND SUBSTANCES

Energy Drinks

Energy drinks can be dangerous for teenagers if they drink them often. Even though many say they are natural, they aren't. Energy drinks also have a lot of sugar and caffeine, which can be bad for your health in the long run.

Without doing a lot of research, it's hard to say whether it's safe for teens to drink energy drinks every day, before or after a sport or activity. So instead of making it a habit to drink energy drinks from the store, focus on drinks with natural ingredients that boost energy and keep sugar levels stable. Here is some information about possible negative effects that can happen when teenagers drink energy drinks.

Types of Energy Drinks

There are two kinds of energy drinks, the ones that come in bottles or cans and the ones that come in smaller bottles, like shots.

In both groups, caffeine is one of the main ingredients. The American Academy of Pediatrics says that energy drinks have a lot of caffeine and other stimulants that should not be a regular part of a teenager's diet.

The Side Effects of Energy Drinks

The U.S. National Center for Complementary and Integrative Health says that teenagers' health could get worse if they drink energy drinks. Energy drinks can be bad for teens' health because they have a lot of caffeine and other chemicals.

Here are some bad things that can happen if you drink energy drinks often:

A report says that teens who drink energy drinks often might have trouble sleeping, learn less, and do worse in school.

There could be a higher chance that they will use drugs, smoke cigarettes, or drink alcohol.

Shobha Bhaskar, a pediatric hospitalist at St. Louis Children's Hospital, says that energy drinks are not very healthy because they don't have much nutrition, have a lot of sugar, and a lot of caffeine. Teenagers might get sick if they drink these drinks often.

Chapman University research shows that 40% of thirteen- to nineteen-year-olds who drink energy drinks have side effects like insomnia, nausea and vomiting, jitteriness, headaches, and stomach pain. In extreme situations, the teen might have seizures.

The National Institutes of Health says that drinking a lot of energy drinks may make it hard to sleep and may also make people more likely to take risks (drug use, tobacco use, fighting).

Energy drinks have different amounts of guarana, caffeine, creatine, ginseng, taurine, vitamins, protein, carbs, amino acids, and minerals. Caffeine, which makes you pee, can make you lose water if you mix these substances with it.

The University of Utah says that energy drinks may have more than 500mg of caffeine, which is the same as drinking fourteen cans of caffeinated soda. When this much caffeine is taken into the body, it can lead to caffeine toxicity.

Some energy drinks could have alcohol in them. Due to a ban by the U.S. Food and Drug Administration, caffeine and other stimulants are not added to alcoholic energy drinks. But these drinks are still called "energy drinks," even though they have been changed so that there are no more stimulants in them.

Note that these side effects are more likely to happen if the teen consumes energy drinks often. A can of it every so often might not be a big deal.

Essentially, it's a good idea to stick to other forms of hydration and energy boosts! Make sure you have a good sleep routine, eat a healthy diet, and keep active. All of these things are a more natural way to boost your energy.

Supplements

There is no reason for you to take any form of supplement unless your doctor has prescribed it. With your regular diet, you should be getting all you need to maintain a healthy lifestyle.

If you're concerned about something, or maybe things just feel "off," talk with a trusted adult and your doctor. There may be other options than supplements, but the main thing is to figure out what's going on first, then develop a plan to fix it.

Drugs and Alcohol

The pressure to try drugs and alcohol starts young. And, it can be hard to say no when your friends are all experimenting with these things. The fact of the matter is that the sooner you try these things, the harder it might be to stop.

There is a reason drugs are illegal. Some of the effects aren't noticed until you're already addicted, or you have irreversible health effects. While it may seem like a great idea to forget everything for a while, whatever you're trying to escape will still be there when you come off your high. This is why people continue to use drugs. If they're always living in an "altered state," they don't have to face the scary and hurtful things going on around them.

Instead of falling into this trap, use some of the tips you read earlier and work on creating open communication with someone you trust. Consider therapy if you need it, meditate, whatever you need to do to process the things happening in your life, rather than trying to hide from them.

This can be hard, and it's certainly not easy to do all by yourself. But learning how to handle the tough times is one of the best lessons you can learn in life!

Besides being illegal until you're twenty-one, the same issues occur with alcohol. Even adults have a hard time controlling their addiction. The same thing can be said for when you're younger too.

Peer Pressure

We've talked a lot about peer pressure and standing up for what you believe is right, as well as staying true to yourself.

It should be said that saying those things is often quite easier than doing those things. You will experience times when you feel all alone. These times will cause tears and anger. It will seem like it's just easier to go along with the crowd, even if it doesn't feel right in your gut.

Something important to learn, and it's a hard lesson, is that along your path of life — YOU are your team. You're the one constant who will always be by your side. Friends will come and go...even if you think you'll be friends forever. Boyfriends and girlfriends will come and go as well. It's you that you have to answer to. If you're not happy with yourself, that's an issue.

Learning to love and rely on yourself is essential no matter what age you are.

CHAPTER SIX:
GENERAL KNOWLEDGE

BASIC SEWING SKILLS

There may come a time when you need to know how to hem your pants or sew on a button. Having this skill is fantastic if you shop at thrift stores a lot!

Gather everything you need. Straight pins, an iron and ironing board, a measuring tape or ruler, scissors, a needle, and thread in the same color as your pants are all necessary supplies.

Take off the initial hem. You might need to cut off the original hem of the pants, depending on their length and fabric quality. After unraveling the pants and ironing them flat, use a seam ripper to remove all of the stitches.

Pinch the folds. Invert the pair of pants. To the appropriate length, fold up each pant leg. Place straight pins parallel to the new hem along the top of the fold to secure it in place. You can now put the pants on to make sure they are the appropriate length. Make changes as necessary.

Trim and iron. Each pant leg's folded hem should be ironed to make a crease. Remove the pins and unfold the pant legs once you have a crease. Trim the pants with scissors and a ruler or measuring tape, leaving one inch of extra fabric below the crease. This is known as the "seam allowance" or "hem allowance."

Fold again and pin. Fold up half an inch starting at the raw edge of the pant leg opening and iron as usual. Fold the raw edge over once more and up an additional half inch to keep it from fraying. Once more, pin and iron.

Sew. Use a blind stitch to sew the new hem; this kind of stitch is barely perceptible from the outside of the pants. At the end of the thread, knot it and thread a needle. The knot should be on the inside of the crease as you pull the needle through the seam allowance. Then, re-puncture the seam allowance with the needle. Pull a few threads from the fabric of the pants just behind the seam allowance with the needle before using it to pick up more. This kind of fine stitching should be done all the way around the hem. Finish off with one more secret knot.

Reapply iron. To maintain the crease in your jeans, iron them a second time. Turn them upside down.

Hemming Pants without Sewing

Hem tape, which is available at most drugstores, can be used to hem your jeans if you don't have a sewing machine or needle and thread. When using hem tape, fold your jeans to the appropriate length inside out, pin and iron the crease, and then press the hem tape onto the fold. Iron the folded edge over. Hem tape is only intended to last through a few washings, so it is simply a short-term fix. Lacking an iron? Look for hemming stickers that can be applied without the use of heat.

Fixing a Loose Button

Keep your button close by in case it comes off or becomes loose while you're out and about. When you have a moment, gather your button, scissors, a thin sewing needle, and thread. Then take these steps:

Make a knot at the end after threading the needle, making sure that both ends are the same length. Make a strong knot out of the two ends that is big enough to prevent it from slipping through the fabric.

Make an Anchor Point: You must make the button's anchor in the form of an "X." Start by inserting the needle into the front and back of the fabric. By passing the needle from the front to the back of the fabric, make a little diagonal line. To make the "X," repeat this procedure one more time.

Place the Button: To lift the button from the fabric, slide a straight pin or toothpick beneath the "X" and over the button. Sew the button in place with as many stitches as necessary, beginning from the fabric's back. Instead of sewing the thread in a crisscross pattern, sew it in two distinct loops to keep the stitching level and help prevent fraying.

Create the Shank: This is done by pushing the needle up through the fabric rather than the button on your final stitch. To create the "shank," remove the pin or toothpick and wind your thread around the threads securing the button to the fabric. To knot off the button, pull firmly and then pierce the fabric at the rear with the needle.

For the fabric to sit between the button and the garment when the garment is buttoned, shanks are required.

Tie the Thread: On the fabric's reverse, tie a little knot. Once you've tied a knot, tighten it up and trim the extra thread.

COOKING BASICS

The following basics are just the beginning. Knowing how to cook is one of life's must-have skills. You don't have to be a master chef, but you should be able to feed yourself.

Boil Water

Making pasta, hard-boiled eggs, or cooked potatoes all start with boiling water, a seemingly easy process. There are numerous things you won't be able to make or accomplish if you don't know how to boil water.

- Prepare a pot with water.
- Set on a stove with high heat.
- Allow the water to fully become a rolling boil. It will clearly be bubbling at this point.
- The amount of water to use is one thing we don't frequently consider. You must account for what you are adding to the pot and leave space for it to be added without causing the water to spill or boil over.
- Another thing to keep in mind is that covering a pot with a lid will trap heat, causing the water to boil more

quickly. Additionally, adding salt to the water will lower its boiling point and hasten the process of evaporation.

Boil an Egg

The major issue with boiling eggs is that people frequently overcook them, resulting in a dark green color around the yolk.

In the bottom of a saucepan, arrange the eggs in a single layer. Pour at least two inches of cold water over the eggs.

Bring to a rolling, full boil. If an egg does crack while cooking, adding a teaspoon of vinegar to the water could prevent the egg whites from spilling out. Additionally, adding 1/2 teaspoon of salt to the water makes it simpler to peel the eggs and prevents cracking.

Reduce the heat and simmer for ten to twelve minutes.

Drain the water immediately, then fast cool by rinsing with cold water. The eggs are unable to continue cooking as a result.

Freezing Hamburgers (or anything else)

The following freezing methods also apply to other items that you might freeze in addition to hamburgers.

Make sure the things you purchase from the store are not rotten, sealed, or expired as your first step. You shouldn't purchase hamburger if it doesn't appear brilliant red.

At home, divide the meat into amounts that are appropriate for each recipe. In most instances, you won't need more than a pound for a recipe.

Wrap each quantity separately using foil, freezer paper, or plastic wrap. Place in freezer bags measuring one gallon, pressing out all the air before closing or store them in a glass freezer-safe, air-tight container.

Label the item with dates, amounts, the nature of the item, and other significant information. If you are freezing a recipe, it's a good idea to note the cooking temperatures and times on the label.

Defrosting Frozen Meat

A few methods can be used to thaw frozen meat. You might choose one based on how much time you have until you need the meat because some demand more time than others.

In the fridge, place the meat on a plate to catch any liquid that may leak while it thaws in the refrigerator. Let it thaw for twenty-four hours.

To thaw in cold water, place the bagged item in the sink and submerge it in water to thaw. Use water that is lukewarm to chilly. Bacteria can grow in hot water environments. Until the meat has thawed, change the water approximately every thirty minutes.

For the microwave, remove all the packaging and set the frozen food on a microwave-safe dish to thaw. The beef can be defrosted using the microwave's defrost setting. Cook immediately after that.

Using Chicken

To be safely cooked through, most meats, including chicken, must reach an internal temperature of 165 degrees Fahrenheit. The thermometer should be placed into the thickest section of the thigh when roasting a complete bird, but it shouldn't touch the bone.

Keep in mind that simply glancing at meat won't tell you whether it's safely cooked. Pork is one type of cooked, uncured red meat that can still be pink even after reaching a safe internal temperature.

Pan-fried - On medium heat, you can pan-fry chicken in either oil or water. Use one or two tablespoons of oil (enough to just cover the bottom of your frying pan). Water requires more since it boils off more quickly. Thus, applying just enough to cover the pan with a thin layer would be appropriate.

The chicken can also be seasoned or marinated before frying. Purchasing a spice packet or marinade bottle from the supermarket and following the instructions is a simple method to accomplish this.

To ensure that the chicken is cooked through, use a thermometer to check the internal temperature of the meat.

Grill - You can also grill, or air fry your chicken following any recipe you might find on Pinterest, TikTok, or YouTube. The main thing is to make sure it is fully cooked before eating.

Steaming Vegetables

Vegetables should be cut into consistent sizes, and steaming should not be done for too long.

To ensure that the vegetables cook at roughly the same rate and that they are all finished at the same time, cut them into consistent sizes.

Veggies can be combined, but keep in mind that softer vegetables, like broccoli, will cook more quickly than more dense vegetables, like carrots. When steaming a mixture of vegetables, add the slower-cooking vegetables first and the faster-cooking vegetables after a few minutes.

In order for the denser veggies to cook more rapidly and finish at the same time as the other vegetables, you can also cut them somewhat smaller.

Set the timer for three minutes in the beginning and check it periodically, so you don't over steam.

Vegetable Steaming Time

- Arugula and spinach: 3 minutes
- Peas: 3 minutes
- Green beans, cauliflower, and broccoli florets: 5 to 7 minutes
- Potatoes, Turnips, Squash, and Carrots: 8 to 20 minutes
- Collards and kale: 10 minutes

Make Use of Leftovers

Chicken

- Chop up leftover chicken to use in chicken salad.
- Slice chicken to make sandwiches.
- For quesadillas, combine cheddar cheese shreds with tortillas.
- To prepare chicken pot pie, create or purchase a pie crust.

Ground Beef

- Add it to macaroni and cheese.
- Create a taco salad.
- Add boiled peas and carrots, gravy, and mashed potatoes to make Shepard's pie.
- Make tacos.

Prepared Vegetables

- Whip up a quiche.
- Make veggie soup.
- Prepare a stir-fry using chicken strips.

There are several meal kits you can find at the store that include everything you need. You can find them in the frozen section, as well as in the aisles. Don't be afraid to experiment with ingredients.

WASHING CLOTHES

The first time you do laundry, it can seem like a difficult process. You don't want to end up with pink shirts or shrink-wrapped sweaters, for sure. Follow these tips, and you'll be a laundry guru in no time!

Sort your wardrobe. You may be familiar with this one: separate your clothing by color and material before washing it (lights and darks, delicates). This will make it possible for you to wash garments at the ideal temperatures and with various washing cycles without causing any harm.

Go over the care label. Some clothes are not at all delicate, while others may only be hand washed or dry cleaned. Follow the care recommendations, sort, and wash them. Every item in your washing machine has the ideal program.

Prepare stains. Check for stains before adding clothing to the washing machine. If you pretreat them with a stain remover, they are significantly simpler to get rid of.

Don't overwork the equipment. In order to get the best washing outcomes, clothes require space to move around. Your clothing might not be as clean as it should be if you overload your washing machine.

Pick the appropriate water temperature. Towels, bed linens, kitchen towels, and any other non-delicate clothes can be washed in hot water (between 60 and 95 degrees). For white and light-colored clothing, warm water (40–60°) is ideal, while colored and dark clothing benefits from colder water (30° or less). You can always consult the care label if you're unsure.

Use softener and detergent. Take care not to use too much detergent. The garments are not cleaner with more detergent. To determine the proper dosage, read the directions on the detergent package or, even better, on the washing machine. Add vinegar or fabric softener if you prefer your garments to be extra fluffy and soft.

Don't overfill the washer with damp laundry. After the washing cycle is finished, remove the damp clothing from the washer and dry it as quickly as you can. Otherwise, it can begin to have an unpleasant scent.

DISHWASHING TIPS AND TRICKS

How to hand-wash dishes:

- Remove food from the plates.
- Fill the sink with hot, soapy, clean water.
- Wash and scrub them in water.
- Rinse to remove any suds and debris.
- Dry using a towel or air dry.

Dishwashing soap is typically "diluted" in a sink or dishpan filled with water, or it can be squirted directly onto a sponge or the soiled dish. Regardless of the method you use for dishwashing, follow the instructions on the detergent bottle to use the proper amount. This is especially important with concentrated detergents, which may require less than you think.

Also remember that some equipment, such as baking pans with internal air cushions, should not be submerged in water. For advice, consult the manufacturer's instructions!

Using a Dishwasher

Scrape any extra food off the plates before loading them into the dishwasher, then space the dishes equally apart with the filthy side slanted down toward the water jets to guarantee clean dishes every time. Avoid stacking your containers on top of one another to prevent the water jets from thoroughly cleaning the inside.

Top rack:

- Fill the top rack with items like bowls, cups, mugs, wine glasses, and water bottles.

- Place tiny bowls and plates in between the tines.
- To prevent warping, always put plastic containers and lids on the top rack. Always look at the bottom to ensure that your plasticware is dishwasher safe.

Bottom shelf:

- Large equipment such as dinner plates, serving platters, baking dishes made of stainless steel, dishwasher-safe baking pans, and other significantly soiled dishes should be placed in the bottom rack.
- Place pots and pans toward the dishwasher's back or along the sides.
- Place utensils in the dishwasher's utensil basket while keeping knives and other sharp objects pointed downward to prevent harm.
- Check if anything obstructs the wash arms before shutting the dishwasher door.

Put detergent in the dishwasher.

Although it may vary depending on the model, most detergent dispensers are located on the inside bottom portion of the dishwasher door. To properly dispense detergent into the dishwasher:

- Put detergent in the dispenser for detergent.
- Up until the line indicates full, pour rinse aid into the rinse aid dispenser. If your dishwasher lacks a dedicated rinse aid dispenser, you can buy a rinse aid

basket or use rinse aid-infused detergent pills or packs.

- When the lid clicks shut, tightly close it. The top of the dishwasher opens to combine the detergent and water once the initial pre-wash cycle is finished.

- The effectiveness of your dishwasher depends on the detergent you use. Use a detergent designed exclusively for automatic dishwashers. Detergents come in various forms, including liquid, powder, gels, tablets, and packs. Although tablets and packets eliminate the need for guessing when determining how much detergent to use, the choice of detergent ultimately comes down to personal preference. Fill the dispenser up to the fill line that most models feature when using liquids, powders, or gels.

A dishwasher typically has three cycles: Quick, Normal, and Heavy Duty. Depending on the size of your load and how dirty your dishes are, you should use the appropriate cycle. Use the buttons usually found on the top or front of your dishwasher door to set your cycle.

The quick cycle often utilizes more water, energy, and heat for quick results. When you need to wash some lightly soiled dishes quickly, use this cycle.

The normal cycle is the most popular dishwasher cycle. It gets rid of regular messes without using additional water. Use this cycle for routine loads that aren't very dirty.

The heavy duty cycle will often use more water and higher temperatures to completely clean your cookware for loads that include pots, pans, or other extremely filthy items.

The water should be 120°F when it enters the dishwasher for optimum operation. If the water is too hot, it could make it more difficult to remove baked-on food from plates and pots, while water that is too cold might not clean your dishes as well.

Start the dishwasher.

Before choosing your cycle, closing the dishwasher door, and pushing start, be sure nothing is obstructing the wash arms. A typical load will take up to two and a half hours to complete, but the light on the front or top of your dishwasher should let you know when the cycle is complete.

OTHER HOUSEHOLD BASICS

Changing a Lightbulb

First—shut off the power.

Never try to replace a light bulb while the power is still on. Keep in mind: safety first!

Second—let the lightbulb cool. Keep in mind that light bulbs can be very hot when operating, so wait until they have cooled before touching them.

Fortunately, since LED light bulbs generate little to no heat, you won't have this issue if it is an LED bulb.

Third—remember safety first from step one! In general, light bulbs are located in challenging-to-reach places. This suggests that replacing them with a ladder is usually a good idea.

Last but not least, discard the old lightbulb.

Checking and Changing a Fuse in Your Fusebox

If part of your power suddenly goes out, you might have a blown fuse. Typically, you need to flip the switch to reset it, but you might have to change the fuse completely.

Look in your garage or basement and locate the fuse box. Find a metal box with a door and many glass fuses that screw into sockets inside. Fuse boxes are typically found in attics, basements, garages, and laundry rooms.

Check the utility meter outside your house if you have problems finding your fuse box. Make an effort to follow the wire leading from the meter. Near the point where power enters the house is often where fuse boxes and circuit breakers are found.

Glass fuses that resemble light bulbs can be seen in older homes. Fuses need to be replaced when they blow. On the other hand, circuit breakers are more common in newer homes and only require flipping and resetting.

Unplug the appliances on the blown circuit and turn off the electricity. At the top of the panel, locate a sizable switch and flip it from "On" to "Off." Unplug the appliances that went off when the fuse blew and turn off the main power. This way, when you turn on the main power, it won't overload the new fuse.

If there isn't a main power switch, a sizable block should be seen at the top of the panel. Check for "On" and "Off" labels when you take them out. Reposition it with the "Off" side facing up if it is indicated. Place the block aside while you change the blown fuse if there is no label.

Look for damaged filaments or burned glass in the fuses. Check the panel door's interior to see if there are schematics or labels. If you're lucky, you'll be able to locate the fuse by looking up the room where the power went out. Then, remove the fuse from the socket, counterclockwise twist it, and inspect the glass for any black smudges or frayed filament wires.

Check each fuse separately for burned markings or broken filaments if your fuse box isn't labeled. Label the one you find once it blows! You can eventually have a complete schematic of the fuse box if you name your fuses each time you replace one.

Replace the blown fuse with a new one of equal power. On the fuse, look for a number that represents the amp rating.

To be sure you obtain an identical match, make a note of the number or bring the blown fuse with you to the hardware store. The replacement fuse should then be plugged in and locked in place by turning it clockwise.

To test the new fuse, restart the power. After installing the fuse, make sure you have completely unplugged all of your electrical appliances from the faulty circuit. Reinstall the main block or flick the main fuse switch when you're prepared to restart your home's electricity. Next, check the lights or connect your electronic devices to the circuit to test it.

After replacing the fuse, turn off the main power and check that the fuse is securely attached if your devices are still not working.

You may be utilizing more electrical gadgets than the circuit can manage if the fuse blows again soon after you replace it. Reduce your device usage by unplugging non-essential appliances when not in use.

Call a skilled electrician if you're still having trouble identifying the issue. It might mean that the wiring in your house is broken.

TOOLS

Specific tools you should have and know how to use include things like screwdrivers, a hammer, measuring tape, and a level. The best way to get hands-on training is to head to a hardware store and attend a free class. Most of them offer classes every weekend.

You can also watch YouTube or TikTok to learn how to use specific tools—knowing what tools you need and how they will help you figure out several common household repairs.

HANGING SHELVES

Before starting, acquire the necessary equipment and supplies:

- Shelves
- Shelf supports
- Pencil
- Measurement tape
- Level
- Stud detector
- Screws
- Anchors for drywall
- Screwdriver
- Drill (optional)
- Hammer

Consider the Placement

- Choose the location of the shelf before you begin to hang it.
- A good installation place will be able to hold a lot of weight.
- Take into account the shelf's weight and the weight of each item you plan to set on top.
- Use a stud finder to see whether studs are in the location where you wish to hang heavier shelving, a heavy display, or storage goods. Although wall studs provide more strength, you can use drywall anchors if none are present.

Mark the Position

- Ask for help from a friend to support the shelf against the wall. Make sure it is held in a straight line using a standard level, and then lightly mark the wall with a pencil on both ends.
- Place the shelf brackets at the bottom of the shelf against the wall. To know exactly where to place the screws, mark them within the holes.
- Remove the brackets and shelf from the wall. Make sure everything is identified by going through your markings.

Drill Starter Holes

- You do not need a drill for this; it just makes things easier.
- Use a screwdriver or a power drill set to its slowest speed to drill starter holes for the screws in the bracket markings.
- Don't turn the screws until they are all the way in the wall.

Install the Anchors and Brackets

- Take off the screws and place the first bracket. If the shelf is heavy and you can't find a stud, you can put in a wall anchor.
- Put the screws back in the brackets and tighten each one until it is secure.
- Make sure not to tighten the screws too much when putting the brackets in place.
- Take a moment to clean up the dust and pencil marks on the wall.

Hang the Shelf

- Put the shelf on the bracket and make sure it's in the middle.
- If the top of the bracket has holes, you can attach it to the bottom of the shelf by putting screws in the holes and drilling until they are tight. This will stop it from falling or sliding.

UNCLOGGING SINKS
AND TOILETS

This is much easier with a plunger and supplies to unclog stopped-up drains. You do want to be mindful of how many chemicals you use, though, as they can cause damage to your pipes. If you rent, talk with your landlord about what products they suggest.

The proper plunging technique can be found online so you can watch the steps. It's a simple thing to handle but might seem overwhelming at first. If you have continued problems, something else might be going on.

General Tips

These days, it's easy to find a lot of information online, depending on your needs. If you're searching for "tips for unclogging a sink," watch a few videos to get an overall idea. Once you find a channel with easy-to-follow videos, subscribe so you can watch other videos by that person. For many things, the best way to learn is by doing it yourself, but that doesn't mean you can't ask questions along the way.

CONCLUSION

Growing up isn't easy, especially when your support system isn't as big as it could be. In that case, you need to learn a lot on your own and be okay with communicating when you get stuck.

The key is to find someone you can rely on consistently. This doesn't mean that person will agree with everything you want to do, but they will be there to help steer you back onto the right path if need be.

Keep this book close, as it has a lot of valuable tips to help you through your teen years. It also can set you up for success in the future as all of these tips are things you will need for your whole life. From getting that first car loan to making sure you're sleeping enough to cooking your very first meal all by yourself, we've got you covered.

Made in the USA
Coppell, TX
22 February 2023

13244975R00075